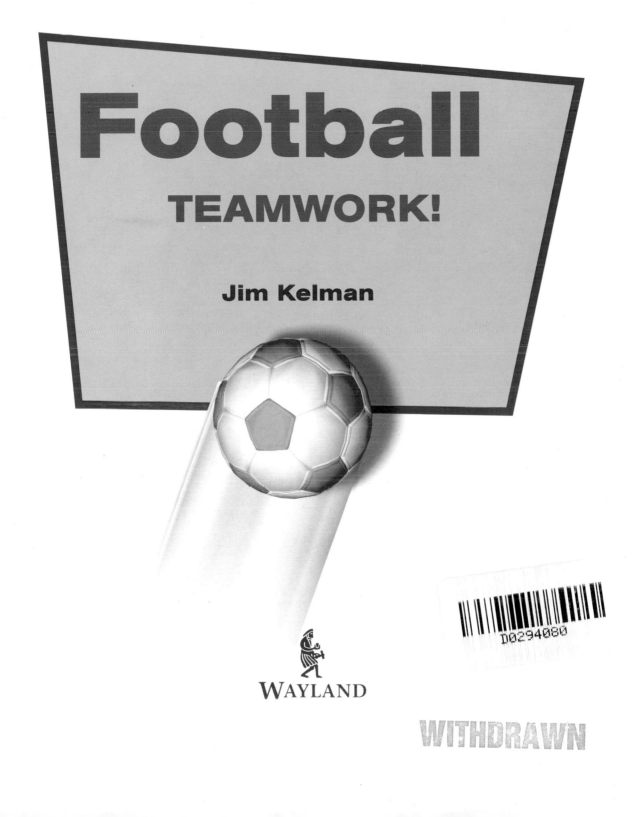

Football

TEAMWORK!

Jim Kelman

WAYLAND

FOOTBALL
Teamwork!
other titles in the series:
Rules of the Game
Skills of the Game
Players and Tactics

Produced for Wayland
Publishers Limited by
Thunderbolt Partnership

Editor: Paula Field
Designer: Eljay Yidirim
Photography: Steve Gorton
Artwork:Phillip Morrison

First published by
Wayland Publishers Limited
61 Western Road, Hove,
East Sussex BN3 1JD
England.

British Library Cataloguing in
Publication Data
Kelman, Jim
Teamwork!. - (Soccer)
1. Soccer - Juvenile literature
1.Title 796 . 3` 34
ISBN 0 7502 2325 1

Printed in Italy by G. Canale &
C.S.p.A.

Contents

Introduction

The players on a football pitch are the main focus of a team because they are the ones who score the goals and win or lose the matches. However, they are just part of a large group of people who work hard behind the scenes to make a football team successful.

▶ Whatever the size of the club the determination to win each game is clear. Each player gives his or her best effort for their team.

◀ The team's strategy is very important. Everyone has a job to do and talking it all through before the game starts helps the players work together.

A winning unit

Being in a team means that no one person is more important than another. Each player has their own job to do, but they must also function as a winning team. The tactics of every match are decided by the manager, who makes sure each player knows what to do.

▼ By working as a team, Brazil have won the World Cup four times. But in the 1998 World Cup Final, they relied on just one player, Ronaldo, and lost 3-0 to the host nation, France.

5

Managers and coaches

The manager of a football club is appointed by the chairman. He or she has one major role – looking after the first team.

The manager is responsible for the style of play, the tactics of the team, and for buying and selling players. When a manager goes into the transfer market, he talks to his chairman so that he knows how much money he can spend.

▲ Managers such as Coventry City's Gordon Strachan are as involved in the game as the players. Unfortunately for them, all they can do is watch!

Managers have coaches and assistant coaches to help them at all levels in the club. They will work hard to achieve maximum effort from their players every time they play.

▶ Manchester United's manager Alex Ferguson and his first-team coach Brian Kidd usually go out on the training pitch with their team.

Motivation

Each manager has his own personal way of encouraging his players. There may be financial rewards, trips abroad during the season, and even visits by psychologists and faith healers.

◀ Many managers look abroad for players to buy. It is common for a club like Chelsea to have about 50 per cent of their team made up of foreign players, such as Italian player-manager Gianluca Vialli.

The squad

In order to develop a successful team, managers build up a squad of players. There are usually 18-20 players in a squad, which can be made up of two goalkeepers, three defenders, four wide players, four midfield players, four strikers and two players who can play anywhere.

▲ England bring on squad members Paul Gascoigne and Ian Wright.

▼ The Chelsea squad celebrate winning the 1997 FA Cup.

Keeping fit

The squad of players that the manager assembles are also under the care of the club's fitness trainer and physiotherapist. They make sure that the players keep fit, and also treat them if they are injured.

Injury time

While a player is recovering from an injury – which sometimes takes months – the manager will replace him with another squad player with similar skills. The manager might even give one of the youngsters a chance to play in the first team.

▲ The modern game is very fast and players are liable to be injured, especially when playing at high speed. Sometimes treatment can be given on the field. Other times the injury is too serious and the player has to be carried off for further treatment.

MUSCLE TEARS ARE THE MOST COMMON INJURIES

9

CHOOSING THE TEAM

Before the match, the manager works with the team on tactics and teamwork. They will talk about the opposition's strengths and weaknesses and who the key players are. The manager will pick his team accordingly.

▲ The eleven players who are picked for the first team will have been carefully selected by the manager.

Playing regularly

It is important that the players understand each other, which usually comes from playing together regularly. So the manager will try to pick many of the same players each week.

Communication

Communication plays a large part in the game and the players are always helping each other as different situations occur during the game. The goalkeeper and his defenders always talk to each other. The goalkeeper is in a good position to see what is happening, while the defenders are watching the opponents or the ball.

▲ Goalkeeper Peter Schmeichel calls to his defenders and points to where they should be.

▲ Some players like Liverpool's Steve McManaman use their arms to communicate with their team mates.

Keep it simple

The forward players help each other out by advising when to cross the ball, dribble, pass or shoot. When you communicate with words, keep it short and simple, such as: 'go for goal', 'shoot', 'get closer', 'be there first'.

Systems of play

MARKING SYSTEMS

As well as choosing the team, the manager will decide which marking system the team will use. This is a way of organizing the team so that all the players know who will be marking which attacker. There are two main systems of marking – man-to-man and zonal marking.

Man-to-man marking

This means that each defender in your team marks a particular attacker from the opposing team. The defender will watch this player throughout the game. As the game moves forward towards the penalty area, the defenders must mark their chosen attacker tightly and make it as difficult as possible for the attacker to shoot.

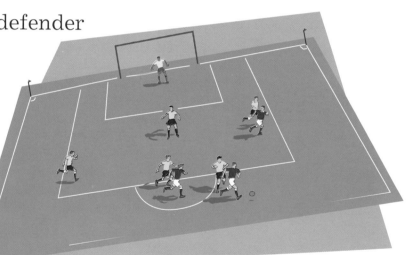

▲ This type of defensive system works best in the defending third as long as there are some spare defensive players to put the attackers under pressure – one player should never be left to mark the opponent who has the ball.

Zonal marking

If the manager decides to use a zonal marking system, you will be responsible for defending an area or zone, rather than just one player. As you move up and down the pitch, the area you are marking moves with you. You will usually mark any opposition player who comes within 5-10 metres of you.

▼ Attacker (1) moves across the defence. Defender (2) marks this attacker until he moves out of his area, when defender (3) takes over.

Mixing systems

Many football teams use a mixture of both systems to make the most of the players they have available. For example, when an opposition attacker is very skilful, one defender might mark him man-to-man, while the rest of the defenders mark zonally.

TEAM FORMATION

The manager will also decide which formation to play. Formation is a word used to describe the shape of the team – where the players are on the pitch.

4-2-4

The 4-2-4 is an attacking system that will give your team at least six players going forward when you have possession.

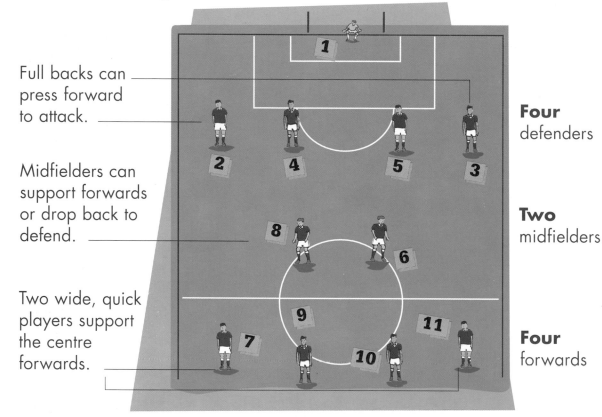

Full backs can press forward to attack.

Midfielders can support forwards or drop back to defend.

Two wide, quick players support the centre forwards.

Four defenders

Two midfielders

Four forwards

The formation the manager chooses depends on which players are in the team, the opposition and whether it will be an attacking or defensive game.

4-3-3

The 4-3-3 system provides a very compact system with seven defensive players when your team has possession and six attacking players when you have won the ball.

Wing backs can move into wide attacking or defensive areas.

Midfielders can make forward or defensive runs.

Three front players create space and give width.

Four defenders

Three midfielders

Three forwards

4-4-2

This system means that the team can maintain a strong defensive position with at least eight players who can get into a defending position.

Two defensive-minded players in wide attacking areas will also go into forward areas to support the centre forwards.

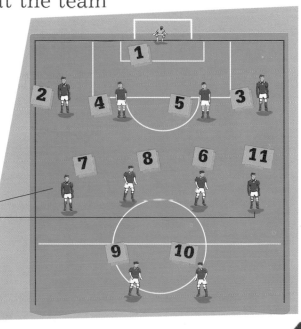

Four defenders

Four midfielders

Two forwards

5-3-2

The 5-3-2 system or 'sweeper' system allows both wing backs to attack, while the sweeper provides cover for the defenders and 'sweeps up' any loose balls. The midfielders can be flexible depending on the type of game – whether it is a home or away match and who the opposition are.

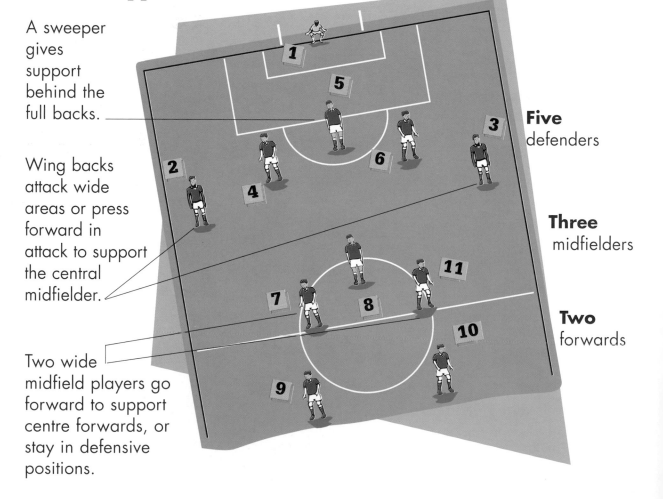

A sweeper gives support behind the full backs.

Wing backs attack wide areas or press forward in attack to support the central midfielder.

Two wide midfield players go forward to support centre forwards, or stay in defensive positions.

Five defenders

Three midfielders

Two forwards

5-2-3

This 5-2-3 system gives the option of having seven attacking players (2,3,8,10,7,9 and 11) or seven defensive players (4,5,6, 2,3,8 and 10). If you have quick forward players who are good at keeping possession, the 5-2-3 system will use their skills.

Two wing backs can come forward (as shown here) to support forwards.

Two midfielders can hold their central positions, come forward to support the attackers or drop back into defence.

Five defenders (includes wing backs)

Two midfielders

Three forwards

The striker and two wide players can swop places with each other to confuse their markers.

17

Set pieces

During the game both teams will use set pieces. Set pieces include throw-ins, corners, free kicks and penalty kicks.

Throw-ins

If the throw-in is in your defensive third, don't throw the ball towards your goal. Throw the ball to a team mate with time and space to play it forward, or throw it forward and close to the sideline.

Receiving the throw

If the throw is in the middle of the pitch or in your attacking third, throw it to someone in space to receive the ball so that they can either cross the ball or run with it and shoot.

▲ Players (1) and (2) do a 'crossover run' to confuse their markers and player (1) runs on to the ball. They have created space and player 1 has time to decide what to do with the ball.

18

Long throws

Some players have the skill to throw the ball a long way. When the throw-in is in the attacking third, it act like a cross. Many goals come from long throws.

▲ Player (1) plays the ball to team mate (2) who has a better view of the goal – this could be an opportunity for a power shot. It is important that players (3) and (4) stay close to the goal area so that they can follow in for rebounds or deflections.

Free kicks

Free kicks can be direct or indirect. Whichever it is, take time to get it right. You may have players who can strike the ball with great accuracy and power.

Bend and swerve

There are some players who can bend and swerve the ball. If the free kick is directly in front of goal then a power shot might be used. If the kick is at an angle, it might be better to use a swerving shot.

Corners

There are three main types of corners - outswingers, inswingers and the short corner. Inswingers are hard to defend against, especially if strong, determined runs are made across the goalkeeper and defenders. If the goalkeeper is very tall an outswinging corner will keep the ball well away from him.

VARY
YOUR
CORNER
KICK
TACTICS

Short corners

A short corner is a good way to build up an attacking move from a set piece. They are ideal if you have players in your team who can dribble with pace into the penalty area. You could get in a cross, score a goal, or even win a penalty.

◀ Player (1) pretends to cross the ball, but instead plays it short to his team mate (2) who has sprinted out of the penalty area. Player (2) quickly returns the ball to player (1) who is free to shoot, cross or dribble the ball towards the goal.

Penalty kicks

If you have to take a penalty, remain calm and focused. Decide how to strike the ball – swerve, power or side foot – and which part of the goal to aim for. You must stick to these decisions and not change your mind at the last minute.

Saving a penalty

If you are the goalkeeper who faces a penalty kick, you must also stay calm. You are permitted to move along the goal line before the ball is kicked, but you must try to out-guess the kicker and dive in the right direction.

▲ David Seaman hits the deck in England's Euro '96 match against Spain. He saved the penalty!

Off-the-pitch football

By the time half time arrives, you will be aware of the strengths and weaknesses of the opposition. It is at this time that your manager will give you advice ready for the second half.

Under pressure

If the team you are playing are putting you under a lot of presssure, then your manager may want to make a tactical change – a fresh player coming on in the second half to change the rhythm of the game. If any of your team have been injured then a change will be made to protect them from further injury.

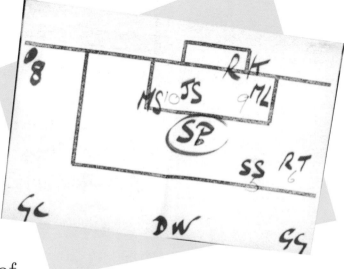

▲ Half time is often a good time to change tactics. Your manager or coach may illustrate what he wants you to do by drawing simple diagrams.

Lifting the spirits

At half time if your team is playing with low motivation, then your manager will try and lift your spirits for the second half.

AWARDS

There is a Fair Play system in operation which publishes league tables showing the fairest team, based on the amount of bookings and sendings off received during the season. If clubs get a poor status and have players who are regularly sent off, the Football Association can call them to appear before a committee to explain the reasons.

Good behaviour

In some Fair Play leagues, the actions of players and supporters are published. At the end of the season Fair Play awards are given to the winning clubs.

▲ At the end of a game, players from both teams usually shake hands with each other to show their appreciation and sometimes swop their shirts.

▶ A Man of the Match award is presented at the end of each game, usually by the sponsors of the match.

Behind the scenes

When you watch a really big match live or on television, have you ever noticed how perfect the pitch looks? All pitches, even your school pitch, have to be looked after.

Grass care

Wherever there are bald patches, the grass is treated with fertilizer and new grass seed is sown. Large bare areas are re-turfed. Some clubs have a drainage system to stop the pitch becoming water-logged, others have undersoil heating systems to prevent the pitch from freezing.

▲ The net and the goal posts are taken down after every match to be repaired and stored away safely.

THE STADIUM

Most modern stadiums are all-seater, with most of the seats covered by grandstands that keep the supporters dry while they watch the game.

▼ Large stadiums, like Wembley, have fantastic facilities and can seat up to 80,000 spectators in comfort.

▲ All League clubs must hold a 'Safety at Sports Grounds Act' certificate. This means that the club's facilites must provide for disabled fans, female supporters and family groups.

Safety first

Lots of clubs also have family areas to make it safer for children to watch the game. Many major clubs have security cameras, which means problems can be sorted out quickly so that fans can watch the game without any trouble.

SUPPORTERS

Most football clubs have supporters that go to every match. These fans usually buy a season ticket so that they have a seat for every game. Other people may only go to one or two matches. Some even support more than one team.

▲ ▶ Fans from all over the world paint their faces in their team colours, like these Brazil and England fans.

Good-natured rivalry

When you arrive at the stadium, there is always rivalry between the two sets of fans. Years ago there was lots of violence and fighting at football matches. This made watching football matches a very bad experience for many supporters.

▶ Even the smallest fans get involved in supporting their team and mascots come in all sizes.

ALL CLUBS HAVE STRICT CODES OF CONDUCT FOR FANS

A pleasure to watch

Nowadays, with the cameras and security plus the all-seater stadiums and the general good nature of football fans, it is a pleasure to be at a big match. Opposing fans mix together before and after the match, but are usually separated during the game itself.

International football

Football is played throughout the world and is governed by an organization called FIFA (*Federation Internationale de Football Associations*). There are 198 members, which are divided into six confederations: Africa, Asia, Concacaf (North & Central America and the Caribbean), Europe, South America and Oceania.

European football

In Europe the confederation is called UEFA (*The Union of European Football Associations*) and is responsible for the European Championships. This competition takes place every four years – two years after each World Cup – and is hosted by a different nation each time.

▲ Germany's team captain Jurgen Klinsmann lifts the 1996 European Championship trophy after beating the Czech Republic 2-1.

THE WORLD CUP

Once every four years, we also witness the biggest sporting event in the world – the World Cup. Countries from the six confederations play a series of qualifying matches to decide which country are truly World Champions.

The host nation

Countries from all over the world bid to be the host nation - this gives them the right to stage the Word Cup finals. It is a great honour to host the finals, but needs enormous amounts of organization to entertain teams and fans from every part of the planet.

▲ The World Cup is the most famous trophy in the world and playing in a World Cup tournament is the highlight of every footballer's career.

29

Glossary

All seater stadiums A stadium where every supporter has a seat.

Chairman The head of the club, who appoints the manager and makes money for the club.

Communication When players help and advise each other during a match.

CONCACAF An organization that governs the football played in North and Central America and the Caribbean.

European Cup A tournament that takes place every four years and involves all European countries.

Fair Play system A league that lists the fairest teams in each football league and awards a trophy at the end of the season.

FIFA An organization that governs the football played around the world.

Long throws A set piece which involves throwing the ball a long way on to the pitch.

Manager The person who picks the team and looks after the players.

Man of the Match An award presented to the best player on the pitch.

Man-to-man marking When a defender marks a particular attacker for the whole game.

Marking systems The way in which a team defends – either man-to-man marking or zonal marking.

Physiotherapist A person who looks after injured players and treats their injuries with massage or medicines.

Safety at Sports Grounds Act An Act of Parliament that ensures the ground is safe and provides facilities for all supporters.

Season ticket A book of tickets which ensures the supporter gets the same seat at every home match.

Set pieces Throw-ins, corners, free kicks and penalty kicks are all set-pieces. Most teams practice different ways of taking set pieces at training.

Short corner A set-piece which involves two or more players taking a free kick from the corner circle.

Sponsors Companies and organizations that give football clubs money in return for advertising their name on the team shirts or in the stadium.

Squad The players that the manager can choose from to play in a match.

Supporters People who pay to go to football matches and support the club.

Suspended player A player who is unable to play a game because he has received a red card and has been banned as a punishment.

Systems of play The shape of the team and the marking system it uses.

UEFA The organization that governs all the football played in European countries.

World Cup A tournament that takes place every four years and involves 32 countries from throughout the world.

Zonal marking When defenders mark an area, rather than a single player.

Further information

Football Associations

English F.A. 9 Wyllyotts Place, Potters Bar, Herts ENJ 2JD.
Irish F.A. 20 Windsor Ave, Belfast BT9 6EG.
F.A. of Ireland 80 Merrion Sq South, Dublin 2, Eire.
Scottish F.A. 6 Park Gardens, Glasgow G3 7YF.
Welsh F.A. Plymouth Chambers, 3 Westgate St, Cardiff CF1 1DD.

Books

World Cup Pocket Annual Bruce Smith (Virgin Publishing) 1998

Websites

442 Website http://virgin.net/442

Videos

The Exclusive World Cup Video Collection (Crazy Eddy's) 1998
Hope and Glory: The Official History of the England Football Team
(Vision Video) 1998

Computer Games

World Cup Semi-Final/World League Soccer (Playstation)
Sony Computer Entertainment 1998

Music

The Best Footie Anthems in the World - Ever! (Virgin)1998
Allez! Ola! Olé! Music of the World Cup
(Sony Music T.V.)1998

PICTURE CREDITS:
Tony Williams Publications: pp.4t,10,22,23,25b.27.
Allsport U.K. Ltd. pp.5,6,7b,8,9,11,21,24,25t,26,28,29.

Index